Not Soup,
But Great Mulligan Stew

Something for Everyone

food for the soul

Bernadette Sharkey

Tellwell Talent
www.tellwell.ca

ISBN
978-0-2288-6066-2 (Paperback)
978-0-2288-6067-9 (eBook)

Table of Contents

Chapter 1

Wise Words and
Points to Ponder

What if you had to choose to live as though it was your last day on earth? How would you live it? Would you choose to be more loving or maybe forgive and forget more easily? Would you give more generously or speak more kindly? We must remember that yesterday has passed away, tomorrow is not promised, but today is here! We need to choose to use today wisely and understand this; everything that is not of an eternal nature, is useless to us! It would also benefit us to keep in mind that the end of this "life" is only the beginning!

We've all heard the saying "Faith can move a mountain", but have you heard that "Love can move a heart?"

Don't be quick to judge someone just because they sin differently than you, but instead keep in mind, anyone who knows the right thing to do, but fails to do it...is sinning. As Iyanla Vanzant puts it; "Live your life with purpose and the rest of your life will be the very best of your life!"

We are going to continue bleeding and hurting until the deepest of our wounds are healed. We can temporarily stop, or slow the bleeding with bandages like drugs, gambling, alcohol, work, sex or a mountain of other things, but the pain will always find its way to the surface and ooze through again, only to need a new bandage. Instead, if we can find strength in our weakness, reach deep inside the wound and pull out the root of that pain, then our past memories won't be able to keep us in bondage anymore and we can finally feel peace.
- Bernadette S

Over the years, certain quotes and pieces of scripture have really touched my heart and encouraged me. I have chosen some that I would like to share with you! I pray you find comfort, encouragement and delight in them!

"Things happen around you and things happen to you, but the most important are the things that happen in you."
- *Les Brown*

"Make a habit to hang around with 'O Q P's', *only quality people.*"
- *Berni Sharkey*

"If you are the smartest person in your group, you need to find a new group."
- *Confucius*

"There are only four things you need to do with a Bible. Read it, meditate on it, speak it, obey it."
- *Lectio Divina*

"There are three things that cannot be hidden for long. The sun, the moon, and the truth."
- *Buddhist Quote*

"Sometimes a fish doesn't know how much he likes the water until he finds himself on the bank."
- *Unknown*

"It is not what a person knows that counts, but it is what he does with what he knows that counts."
- *Unknown*

"Every word we speak can be a brick to build on or bulldozer to destroy. Be conscious of what you say and how you say it."
- *Unknown*

"Be careful what you think because your thoughts run your life."
- *Proverbs 4:23 NCV*

"The way of a fool is right in his own eyes, but he who listens to counsel is wise."
- *Proverbs 12: 15 AKJV*

"Be not wise in your own eyes."
- *Proverbs 3: 7A NIV*

"People with understanding control their anger; a hot temper shows great foolishness. A peaceful heart leads to a healthy body."
- *Proverbs 14:29-30 NIV*

"Everyone should be quick to listen, slow to speak and slow to become angry..."
- *James 1:19 NIV*

I thoroughly enjoyed Rick Warren's book, "The Purpose Driven Life", I found it was full of insight and wisdom. Here are some excerpts that have really stuck with me.

"Don't repress it-confess it, don't conceal it-reveal it."

"Revealing your feeling is the beginning of healing."

"Great opportunities often disguise themselves as small tasks."

"What happens outwardly in your life is not as important as what happens inside of you."

"If God used only perfect people nothing would ever get done."

"Character is both developed and revealed by tests, and all of life is a test."

- Rick Warren, The Purpose Driven Life

"Learn to 'doubt your doubts and believe your beliefs.'"
- Dieter F. Uchtdorf

"The greatest gift you can give someone is your time."
- John Mulhall, Geddy's Moon

"You may be disappointed if you fail, but you are doomed if you don't try."
- Beverly Sills, Quotable Quotes, Readers Digest

"Humility is not thinking less of yourself, but thinking of yourself less."
- C.S. Lewis

"If you wait for perfect conditions, you will never get anything done."
- Ecclesiastes 11:4 (paraphrased)

"The truth will set you free, but first it may make you miserable."
- *James A. Garfield*

"In resolving conflict, how you say it, is just as important as what you say."
- *Unknown*

"The greatest of all art, is the art of living together."
- *William Lyon Phelps, Quotable Quotes, Readers digest*

"You may give gifts without caring, but you can't care without giving."
- *Frank A Clark, Quotable Quotes, Readers Digest*

"Never hesitate to hold out your hand; never hesitate to accept the outstretched hand of another."
- *Pope John XXlll*

"It takes as much courage to have tried and failed as it does to have tried and succeeded."
- *Anne Morrow Lindbergh*

"Storms make trees take deeper roots."
- *Dolly Parton*

"The most important things in life aren't things."
- *Anthony J. D'Angelo*

"Once you can read, all worlds are open to you."
- *Sister Wendy Beckett, Sister Wendy's Odyssey*

"As we grow old, the beauty steals inward."
- *Ralph Waldo Emerson*

"We do not remember days, we remember moments."
-*Cesar Paves*

"Patience! The windmill never strays in search of the wind."
- *Andy J Sklivis, Treasury of Wit and Wisdom*

"To know what is right and not do it is the worst cowardice."
- *Confucius*

"Change your thoughts and you change your world."
- *Norman Vincent Peale, The Power of Positive Thinking*

"There is a time to let things happen and a time to make things happen."
- *Hugh Prather, Treasury of Wit and Wisdom*

"I don't think of all the misery, but of the beauty that still remains."
- *Anne Frank*

"Laughter translates into any language."
- *Graffiti*

"We never know the love of a parent until we become parents ourselves."
- *Henry Ward Beecher, Treasury of Wit and Wisdom*

"Few things are more delightful than grandchildren fighting over your lap."
- *Doug Larsen, Treasury of Wit and Wisdom*

"One filled with joy preaches without preaching."
- *Mother Teresa of Calcutta*

"If you want others to be happy, practice compassion; if you want to be happy, practice compassion."
- *Dalai Lama*

"He who was caught in a lie is not believed when he tells the truth."
- *Spanish proverb*

"Cheerfulness, like spring, opens all the blossoms of the inward man."
- *Jean Paul Richter*

"If you don't want anyone to know, don't do it."
- *Chinese proverb*

"Be patient with everyone, but above all, with yourself
- *St Francis De Sales*

"Spending time with God puts everything else in perspective."
- *Matthew 6:33, (Paraphrased)*

"Tomorrow's world will be shaped by what we teach our children today."
- *Suzanne Woods Fisher*

"Never measure God's unlimited power by your limited expectations."
- *Unknown*

"There is no better test of a man's integrity than his behaviour when he's wrong."
- *Marvin Williams*

"To multiply your joy, count your blessings."
- *J.B. Priestley*

"When we think we are humble, we are not."
- *Unknown*

"Great opportunities to help others seldom come, but small ones surround us every day."
- *Sally Koch, Treasury of Wit and Wisdom*

"It is one of the beautiful compensations of this life that no one can sincerely try to help another without helping himself."
- *Charles D Warner, Treasury of Wit and Wisdom*

"We ourselves feel that what we are doing is just a drop in the ocean, but the ocean would be less because of that missing drop."
-*Mother Teresa, of Calcutta*

"The Golden rule of Friendship: listen to others as you would have them listen to You"
- *David Ausburger, Quotable Quotes, Readers Digest*

"See everything, overlook much, correct a little."
- *Pope John XX 111*

"No one can make you feel inferior without your consent."
- *Eleanor Roosevelt*

"Peace is when time doesn't matter as it passes by."
- *Marie Schell, Treasury of Wit and Wisdom*

"Here is the test to find whether your mission on earth is finished; If you're alive, it isn't.
- *Richard Bach, Treasury of Wit and Wisdom*

"If you can't see God in all, you can't see God at all."
- *Unknown*

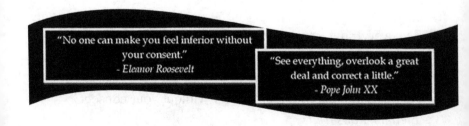

"No one can make you feel inferior without your consent."
- *Eleanor Roosevelt*

"See everything, overlook a great deal and correct a little."
- *Pope John XX*

Chapter 2

The Seven Best
Beauty Tips

by Audrey Hepburn

#1 **For lovely lips-** speak words of kindness.

#2 **For lovely eyes-** seek out the good in people.

#3 **For a slim figure-** share your food with the hungry.

#4 **For beautiful hair-** let a child run their fingers through it once a day.

#5 **For poise -** walk with the knowledge that you never walk alone.

#6 **Don't forget -** people even more than things, have to be restored, renewed, revived, reclaimed and redeemed. *Never* throw out anyone!

#7 **Remember-** if you ever need a helping hand you will find one at the end of each arm. As you grow older you will discover that you have two hands, one for helping yourself, the other for helping others.

The beauty of a woman is not the clothes she wears, the figure she carries, or the way she combs her hair. The beauty of a woman must be seen from in her eyes, because this is the doorway to her heart, the place where love resides.

Audrey Hepburn *(May 4 1929-January 20 1993)*

"Since God made us originals, why stoop to being a copy."
- *Rev. Billy Graham*

"We can't help everyone, but everyone can help someone."
- *Ronald Reagan*

Chapter 3

<u>Published and</u> <u>Unpublished Songs</u> <u>and Poetry</u>

The following songs and poems have been made up, over many years, by both friends and family!

I feel honoured to be able to share them with you!

Thank you, all of you who contributed, your permission is so appreciated! Please know that you have not only blessed me but will also be a true blessing to others!

<u>Winter White</u>

I used to think
That snow was white
And then I saw
It blue one night.
I saw gold one day
With purple shadows and with grey
And then one morning
It was pink!
Now I don't know what to think.

- My Late Nephew Derrick Hennig, age 10

<u>Because You Love Me</u>

You don't see my sin, only my salvation,
And give me an invitation,
to love you too.
You're blinded to all my faults because
I'm already forgiven,
And you love it when I choose to be livin' for you.
How could I deny all you've shown me on this journey?
I've learned I'm not asked to be your attorney,
But as your witness-to shine.
How could I not rely on the fullness
of love that you gave me,
And the freedom to truly just be me
Rather than lie.
How did I think at one time it seemed so crazy?
When it was really just me being lazy,
and running away.
I'm so thankful now that I see, that
it's all a lifelong rehearsal,
That stage is universal, and I can be free.

-Robin L. McDonald (My Daughter)

<u>My Friend</u>

I found a friend a while ago, a friend so tried and true,
we'd laugh and run and soak the sun, under the sky so blue.

And when the snow began to fall and
coldness seemed to hover,
my friend would lead me on and on,
until I could find some cover.
We'll travel on, my friend and I, as far as we can go,
but I may stop and visit folk, if the winds begin to blow.

And if my visit becomes prolonged,
my friend will always wait,
cuz no matter where we go, we'll never be too late.

So, with adventure we shall go, wherever it pleases me,
up a hill, around a bend, to any named city.

So, on and on I shall trudge, whether be night or day,
with my friend, my friend so true,
our most beloved highway.

- Berni Sharkey

<u>Sincerely Yours</u>

Lord, I take my pen to write you a letter
Knowing even now you know what's on my mind
But I think perhaps it might make me feel better
If I see myself here written in a line
And as I close, I see a phrase I took for granted
And it leaps out as I see it written there
And as the truth of it begins to become planted
These two words have now become my heartfelt prayer
Sincerely yours
Lord I signed my life to you
Sincerely yours
With a strong and honest wish
To be the best that I can be at what I am
Without a thought for me
Lord, teach me how to be
Sincerely yours
Without a proud or selfish line
Sincerely yours
From now until there is no time
Please make my life become a letter you can keep
And never throw away, I'll write it till the day
That I become sincerely yours
Sincerely yours
Sincerely yours

- *Unknown*

<u>It's a New Day</u>

It's a new day, a God given day,
So don't go wasting it away.
Start by being thankful, then try being helpful,
And see what God will bring your way.

It's a new day, a God given day,
Lift up your voice to God in praise!
Praise him for His glories; commit to Him your worries,
And let Him guide you all your ways.

It's a new day, a God given day,
So don't go wasting it away,
Praise your Saviour and King, praise Him in everything,
Praise Him, praise Him, come what may.

It's a new day, a God given day,
Surrender your heart to Jesus Christ,
Repent of all your sin, ask your Saviour in,
Accept his gift of everlasting life.

- Berni Sharkey

<u>Care</u>

Spades, diamonds, hearts, clubs,
Trees, flowers, grass, shrubs,
Sky, water, land and air,
What is life if not to care?
Love and hate - they make up life,
Why most of us, we live in strife,
Happiness, there's too little of,
Why can't this world be filled with love?

Faith, hope, love, and trust,
To be happy, they are a must,
Without these things we'll live in hate...
And when we're old, it'll be too late.

- Berni Sharkey

<u>A Love Song</u>

How do I write a love song, which
comes even close to how I feel?
Where do I find these words that could ever begin to reveal?
When you're near me, I forget the
'me' I am when not with you,
I embrace a state of ecstasy that rushes deep, right through.
As I close my eyes and breathe your
breath, a peace of mind sets in,
As a moment now consumes me and I relinquish all to Him.
Relation like I've never known, acceptance without fear,
Even doubt lies far behind, when you whisper in my ear;
"Be still my love, you are my own,
there's nothing you can do,
Nothing more and nothing less, will alter my love for you."
How do you see me without all my faults?
Because YOU are the greatest love song,
You are the great I AM

- Robin L. McDonald (My Daughter)

A Love Poem

Love;
The warmth of joy that emanates deep within
and outward with goose bumps.
Love;
The sweet rush of adrenaline when
a fragment of time in our minds,
is occupied by You.
Love;
The contagious smile can't be wiped off my face
because it literally comes from the heart of my spirit.
Love;
I'm in love with love,
pleasantly addicted!
I never want to spend a day without You.
Love;
For others as much as ourselves.
For ourselves as much as others.

-Robin L. McDonald

<u>If I Were an Icicle</u>

If I were an icicle, I'd sparkle and I shine,
With my very own shape, only one of a kind.
The wind would begin to swirl, sleet would begin to fall;
And inch by inch I'd grow upside down, but tall.
But when the sun comes and I begin to melt,
Disappearing slowly, I'd never forget how that felt.
Now I'm a puddle of water and soon I'll evaporate.
I don't really want to go, but I'll have to cooperate.
"Until next winter" Mr. Rooftop, it's not very far,
But maybe next year I'll hang from a star."

- Paula (McKinley) Sharkey (My Daughter)

<u>My Friend Joe</u>

I'm going to tell you a story, a story sad but true,
It's about my friend who finally found his end,
He found his end in misery.

Now my friend Joe was an okay guy,
all things were going his way,
But then one day he started to play,
The game that led him to misery.

Oh no Joe, I beg you, don't go, you'll
only get yourself in a fix!
Oh Joe, I swear, I know, 'cuz I've been there,
But he turned on my words and went his way.

Now my friend Joe is a needle freak,
and he's happy when he's high,
He owns an arm full of tracks and the clothes on his back,
And this is the way he'll die.

Well, my friend Joe just happens to be
me, and I'm just wasting away,
I'm happy when I'm high, but I know that's a lie,
'Cuz I'm really dying in misery.

- Berni Sharkey

If I Had a Child to Raise over Again

"If I had a child to raise all over again,
I'd finger paint more and finger point less.
I'd do less correcting and more connecting.
I'd take my eyes off my watch, and watch with my eyes.
I would care to know less and know to care more.
I'd take more hikes and fly more kites.
I'd stop playing serious and seriously play.
I'd run through more fields and gaze at more stars.
I'd do more hugging and much less bugging.
I would be firm less often, and affirm much more.
I'd build self-esteem, and the house later.
I'd teach less about the love of power and
more about the power of love."

- Dianna Loomans, From the book "Full Esteem Ahead"
(100 ways to build self-esteem in children and adults.)

<u>**Chant of Labour**</u>

We slug along at work all day; we pound
machines come what may.
In time we put our eight hours in, five
days a week! This must be sin.

Sometimes we're bored, sometimes we're
not, we do our best and try a lot,
To please the boss, come what may, for
Friday noon there is our pay.

A cheque each week we're working for,
nothing less and nothing more,
But it's not as bad as made out to be, for
without our jobs where would we be?

- Berni Sharkey (while working as an assembly line worker)

<u>Years Gone By</u>

There was a time not long ago, when we
were single and don't you know,
That we had fun with drink and smoke, and
we laughed at all those working folk.

Now we are married and getting old, we
have left home and trying to hold
A ten-hour job to make some bread,
to keep a roof over our head.
Yet aren't we now glad to say, we're
like that folk in every way.

- MCR (My Husband)

<u>This Joy</u>

When I first met Jesus as my Lord and
Saviour, I got on my knees to pray
"Father, forgive me; I know I'm a sinner,"
and that's when I heard him say;
You can have my joy for the rest of your life, my
comfort and peace amidst all your strife,
With my Holy Spirit, you'll know it's alright,
to have this joy for the rest of your life.
Well as I got to know Jesus, it made Satan angry,
and he started to send things my way
Like doubts and confusion, discouragement
and trials, and so to my Jesus I'd pray.
"Can I have your joy for the rest of my life, your
comfort and peace amidst all my strife?
With your Holy Spirit I know it's alright, to
have this joy for the rest of my life."
Well as I got older God made me stronger,
friends look at my face and they say,
"What is it about you that made you so
different?" I look at them smile and I say.
"You can have this joy too, for the rest of your life,
this comfort and peace, amidst all your strife,
With His Holy Spirit, you'll know it's alright,
to have this joy for the rest of your life."
You can have this joy too, for the rest of your life,
His comfort and peace amidst your strife
Invite Jesus into your heart and you'll know it's
alright, to have this joy for the rest of your life!

- Berni Sharkey

<u>To Realize</u>

Empty eyes that sink beneath a weather beaten soul
No confidence to cling too misguided thoughts take hold
Believing every lie within her young life she's been told
She cries.
Self-doubt her close companion walks
beside her in deep grief
While the next man just reminds her and nurtures disbelief
That she could ever know true love or ever pain defeat
Soul tied.
Awoken early morning in the middle of the night
A restless voice inside her, significant, yet slight
Plants a seed of new awareness that
will grow into new sight
Fading lies.
The Veil removed exposing new reality of peace
Of love and sanctuary, away from rabid beasts
A place that's not for hiding but a home that gives relief
To realize.
Now walking close behind Him, self-
doubt.... still comes and goes,
But guarded now within righteousness
and a love she'd never known,
In a place outside minds madness that re-ignites her soul
She's alive!

-

Robin L. McDonald

<u>For Grade 12 Grads</u>

Twelve years of reading, writing, spelling,
at times a little overwhelming!
But you've done it "yes sir ree", and now
from books and desks you're free.
What will be next is up to you, choose
wisely child in what you'll do.
For your future seek the Lord, seek His
wisdom as you read His word.
Day by day, year by year, in your heart
of hearts, keep God near.

- Unknown

<u>Marriage</u>

Marriage, what a sacred thing.
It entails much, much more than anyone anticipated!
If we had known even half of the heartaches,
Would we even have considered it?
I DARE SAY YES!
For God sanctifies, God blesses.

- Unknown

When I'm An Old Lady

When I'm an old lady, I'll live with my
kids, and make them so happy,
Just as they did,
I want to pay back all the joy they've
provided, returning each deed,
Oh, they'll be so excited!
I'll write on the wall with reds, whites and
blues, and bounce on the furniture
Wearing my shoes.
I'll drink from the carton and then leave it out,
I'll stuff all the toilets, and oh, how they'll shout.
When they're on the phone and just out of reach,
I'll get into things like sugar and bleach.
Oh, they'll snap their fingers and then shake their head,
And when that's done, I'll hide under the bed.
When they cook dinner and call me to meals,
I'll gag on my okra, spill milk on the table,
And when they get angry, run fast as I'm able.
I'll sit close to the TV, through the channels I'll click,
I'll cross both my eyes to see if they stick.
I'll take off my socks and throw one away,
And play in the mud till the end of the day,
And later in bed I'll lie back and sigh,
and thank God in prayer,
And then close my eyes,
And my kids will look down with a smile slowly creeping,
And say with a groan, "she's so sweet when she's sleeping"

- Unknown

<u>Warm Feeling</u>

A warm feeling in the cold lashing rain
In Him I trust
My secrets
My troubles
Wet pavement felt falling leaves
I felt a friend
My best friend
Caring, He hears what I say
I listen to Him
No storm can take that away

- Paula McKinley, age 14

<u>More Of You</u>

More of You, less of me, that oh Lord is my plea
More of You, less of me
I once was lost, but now am found,
and set up on higher ground
You washed away all my sin, the moment I asked Jesus in
And now I need more of You, less of me
That oh Lord is my plea
To be your servant is my will, your
abundant love my heart to fill
To walk in righteousness and grace, to
know Your heart and seek Your face
I need more of You, less of me
More of You, less of me
More of You, less of me

- Berni Sharkey

<u>A Child's Prayer</u>

Father we thank you for the light
And the blessing of the night
For the rest, the food, and loving care
And all that makes the world so fair
Help us to do the things we should
And to be to others kind and good
In all we do in work and play
To be more loving day by day

- John Flegel (My Father)
1922-2020 Written when he was age 10

To Our Mother: Rose Flegel

Oh Mother we thank thee, from the heart,
for we all know how good thou art,
For the rest, the food, and all the care,
to us you always were so fair.
You helped us to do the things we should,
you were to us so kind and good.
In all we did in work and play, to make us better day by day.
Now I want to thank you for all eight,
before you go, then it's too late.
So, thank you mother before you're gone,
written by your youngest son, John.

- John Flegel,
Written to his mother (My grandmother)
Rose, on behalf of all eight children.

<u>Dearest</u>

Dearest child of God
No matter what the storms of life may be,
Know that God loves you,
And has a wonderful plan for your future.
Listen for His voice,
Trust Him with all your heart,
Let Him guide you to the wonderful
life He has in store for you.
Be like an eagle in a storm, look up and beyond that storm.
There are brighter days.
There are blessings awaiting you,
In His Love.

- Berni Sharkey

The Difference

I got up early one morning and rushed right into the day;
I had so much to accomplish, I didn't take time to pray.
Problems just tumbled about me and heavier came each task
"Why didn't God help me" I wondered.
He answered
"You did not ask"

I wanted to see joy and beauty, but the day toiled on,
Gray and bleak
I wondered why God didn't show me.
He said
"You did not seek"
I tried to come into God's presence; I
used all my keys at the lock.
God so gently and lovely said "my child, you did not knock.

I woke up early this morning, and
paused before entering the day;
I had so much to accomplish that I had to take time to pray.

- Unknown

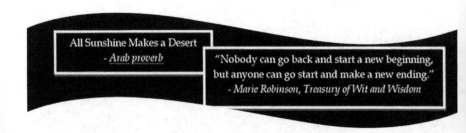

All Sunshine Makes a Desert
- Arab proverb

"Nobody can go back and start a new beginning,
but anyone can go start and make a new ending."
- Marie Robinson, Treasury of Wit and Wisdom

Chapter 4

<u>Tunes for Toddlers</u>

Paddy On The Railroad

Paddy on the railroad, picking up stones.
Along came an engine and broke Paddy's bones.
Oh! Said Paddy, that's not fair!
Oh! Said the engine man, you should'nee been there.

- Sung by Irish Railway workers in the 19th Century

In the memory of Bella Rowe.
Thank you for amusing my three youngsters
with that song. You made it so much fun!

Fishy Fishy

Fishy fishy in the Brook,
Daddy caught him with a hook,
Mommy fried him in a pan,
baby ate it like a man.

- 1868 in "Our Young Folks".

<u>Wee Churtee Birdie</u>

Wee churtee birdie, toe lo lo,
Layed an egg on the windicill,
The windicill began to crack,
Wee churtee birdie roared and grat.
Old Scottish children's poem

- Unknown

<u>My Father Was A Dustman</u>

My father was a dustman, who wore a dustman's cap.
He paid a shilnee ticket to see a football match. The
ball was in the center, the referee's whistle blew, Fatty
took the ball and up the field he flew! Fatty passed
to Skinny and Skinny passed it back. Fatty took a
rotten shot and knocked the goalie flat! But where
was the goalie when the ball was in the net? Half-
way up the goal post, with trousers 'round his neck!
They put him in a stretcher, they put him in a bed,
they fed him castor oil and this is what he said....
    "Ohhhhh! Come on all ye Rangers, never be
afraid, Show them dirty Celtics, how the game is
played. The ball was in the center, the ball was in the
net And all the dirty Celtics, were lying in the wet!"

- Unknown

<u>Fuzzy Wuzzy</u>

Fuzzy Wuzzy was a bear,
Fuzzy Wuzzy had no hair,
Fuzzy Wuzzy wasn't very fuzzy, was he?

- Unknown, Public Domain

<u>Inky Binky Alligator</u>

Inky binky alligator, swimming in the pond,
Along came a sneaky snake, "whomp" the snake is gone,
Along came frisky frog, "whomp" the frog is gone,
And inky binky alligator's still swimming in the pond.

- Mike Sharkey,
Created for his children.

"You are never persuasive when
you are abrasive."
- Rick Warren

Reading is to the mind what exercise is to the
body.
- Quoted by Multiple People!

Chapter 5

Innocent Insights

Kids hardly filter their thoughts, and often, speak them out loud! Before you know, their words go down in history! The next section of quotes, are some cute little quips from our beloved friends & family.

Upon having a lovely pedicure in preparation for attending a summer wedding, my 3 1/2-year-old grandson asked "gramma, when did you get new toes?"
- *Berni Sharkey*

I decided to take my 3-year-old daughter Laura into the bathroom with a few toys while I had a quick shower. Upon exiting the shower and drying off my pleasantly plump body, she said, "Mommy are you ever skinny". I responded, "Thank you, Laura", to which she responded" yes mommy, you sure have a lot of skin!"
- *Faye G. (My Beautiful Late sister)*

My 5-year-old daughter was just beginning to memorize Bible verses. She proceeded to recite Proverbs 18:10 "the name of the Lord is a strong tower, the righteous runneth into it, and is safe." ***Problems*** 18:10.
- *Celeste S.*

God's help is only a prayer away!

My son was misbehaving in church, I whispered to him to stop or I would have to take him out and discipline him. After a few more warnings I picked him up and proceeded to walk up the aisle towards the back of the church, when all of a sudden, he yells, "please pray for me"!
- *Ed H. (My Late Brother in law)*

For those of you who remember the Staples "Easy Button"

My grandson, about two and a half years old at the time was enjoying pressing it over and over, all of a sudden, he handed it to me and asked "Grandma, do you have a hard one?"
- *Berni S.*

I was in church with my grandson and I went to whisper to him to be a little quieter, he replied to me, "Grandma, your voice really smells bad."
- *Violet B.*

Then there is the one about little Johnny, when asked by his mother "why in the world would you put peanut butter on the tires of your tricycle wheels?" Smiling he answered, "so I can have smooth tires."
- *Darlene M. (A dear friend)*

Upon putting an inflatable swimming armband over her feet, little Kate shouted! "Look everyone I'm a mermaid!"
- *Celeste S. (Daughter in Law)*

Bathing her three youngsters (ages 5, 4 and 2) together in the bathtub to save time, the eldest pipes up, mum, we need to get a bigger tub!
- *Celeste S.*

Upon reading a "COVID Santa" poem to my grandchildren, the youngest asked what it really meant, to which the older one answered, you need to make your list really short this year.
- *Mindy M. (Friend)*

Playing Uno with my friend, her daughter-in-law and four-year-old grandson, I called the little guy's mum, "mummy," on several turns. Finally, the little guy looked at me and said," her name is Marfa you know!"
- *Berni S*

Our family goes hunting every fall, so my husband started taking the boys out when they were quite young. When I took my sons to see Bambi and the scene came where Bambi's mother was killed, everyone in the theatre was "ahhing" and then my son calls out "nice shot."
- *Unknown*

Grandchild: How old are you Grandma?
Grandma: Thirty-nine and holding.
Grandchild: How old would you be if you let go grandma?
- *Unknown*

"If you don't "try", you'll never know where the "try" might have taken you!"
- *Unknown*

"There are only three things you can do with money! Give some, save (or invest) some, spend some....
BE WISE!"
-*Unknown*

Chapter 6

Pet Peeves

*I don't think there is anyone on God's green earth
that doesn't have at least one or two pet peeves.
I have canvassed male and female from the ages
of eight to eighty. I have broken them into age
categories, male and female. I hope you enjoy reading
them as much as I enjoyed collecting them.*

<u>Pet Peeves of Young Fellows Ages 8-15</u>
(These are so much fun)

Slow walkers in hallways.
People who talk on and on and on.
People who sing poorly.
A totally clean surface with a smudge.
People who chew with their mouths
open (3 people said this).
People who make loud 'schmucking' sounds while eating.
Having to tie my running shoes.
Hearing "don't forget to brush your teeth" every night.
School. (4 people said this)
Being tickled.
**People who keep sniffing but don't
bother to blow their nose.**
Girls and women who wear too much make-up.

<u>Young Ladies Ages 8-15</u>

Pet walkers who don't pick up after their pets.....Grrrr!
People who have crust in the corner of their lips.
People who chew with their mouths open (5 people said this)
People who don't bother brushing their hair.
Bad makeup job.
Older ladies who still try to dress like they're teenagers.
School.
Dirty fingernails.
Having to get out of my PJ's and getting
dressed on a Saturday morning.
Monday to Friday morning.
Nail Polish that chips off after one day.
**Having to go to bed one hour before
my brother and sister.**
My baby sister getting into my stuff.
Having to eat slightly burned pancakes.
Cold toast.
Being teased.
Being tickled.
Having to do my homework the minute
I get home from school.

<u>Men Ages 16-30</u>

Drivers that cut you off. (5 people)
People who don't use their manners.
Bad parkers in a mall. (2 people)
People wearing dirty clothes when they don't need to.
Impatience.
People who chew with their mouth open. (3 people)
When people don't put my stuff back where they find it.
**When people ask me to do something and
I tell them I can't, then they proceed
to ask me again a few minutes later.**
Older ladies dressing like teenagers. (2 people)
Drunk drivers.
Having to clean the bathroom.
Having to cook for myself.
Waiting for service in a restaurant
when you see free waitresses.
Waiting in a line up for an open cashier.
Waiting in line at the bank.
Homework.
Helping my sister do her chores.

Women Ages 16-30

When people stare at me for a long time.
People who walk really slow.
People who think they know it all.
When girls want guys to do everything for
them and they won't be independent.
When guys think you're incapable.
People who invade your bubble.
People who feel and act like they are entitled.
People who drive slow in the passing lane, grrrr.
Unkemptness.
People who leave their shopping cart in
the parking space beside them.
Having to cook.
Smart asses.
Jerks.
Good movies with really bad endings.
People who interrupt you while you are speaking.
Having to look after my little brother.
Going into a cereal box to have a bowl of
cereal and there are only crumbs left.
Just dribbles left in the milk carton.
Toilet seat left up! (3 people)

<u>Men Ages 31-50</u>

Stupid and inconsiderate drivers.
People who wear odd socks or inside out socks.
Finding unclean dishes that have been
put away in the cupboard.
**People who don't understand what
I'm trying to tell them.**
On the job, when I'm told everything is
ready to go and it's not! Grrr!
People who are sitting daydreaming when
the traffic light has turned green.
When people can't see others POV. (point of view)
When a person holds their fork the
wrong way at the dinner table.
People that don't signal when they're turning
on the corner you're waiting at.
Incessantly barking dogs.
People who think they know everything about everything.
Our government, or lack of.
When people don't acknowledge once you
have allowed them to go in front of you.
People who leave cupboard doors open. (2 people)
Trying to pull those metal tabs off of canned goods.
People who continuously talk about themselves.
People who are constantly late. (4 people)
People who come late for work and think nothing of it.

<u>Women Ages 31-50</u>

Complainers
Stupid drivers (4 people)
Looking after boys or men when they
are sick, they are such babies!
Thistles in my garden.
People who start talking to you when
you're trying to listen to a program.
Bathtub ring. (2 people)
When you meet someone for the first time and
they go on and on talking about themselves.
Shopping carts in the middle of the parking lot. (2 people)
When I'm at a crucial time of cooking a meal
and my company brings me flowers
that need tending, the thought is
lovely, but the timing sucks.
People that don't replace the toilet roll. (5 people)
People who chew with their mouths open. (2 people)
People using spit to clean something or someone.
All injustices.
When boiled eggs don't peel nicely.
Litterers.
Dirty socks lying around.
People who leave the toilet seat UP! (4 people)

<u>(Men & Women) Ages 51 Plus</u>

People who leave cupboard doors open.
Trying to pull those metal tabs off the canned goods.
Plastic produce bags that won't open up
when you are at the grocery store.
Having to wear a mask when I go shopping.
Drivers that are not courteous. (3 people)
People who tailgate me when I'm going the speed limit.
Drivers that are not aware of the vehicle beside them.
People who chew loudly.
Having to bend down to tie my shoes.
Having to cook.
Neighbours having parties into the early AM.
Impatience.
Dirty finger nails.
Undisciplined children.
Having to stand on the bus when there are
youngsters who could offer their seat.
Not seeing my grandchildren as often as I'd like.
Seeing recyclables going in the garbage.

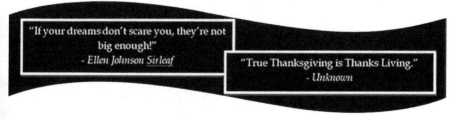

"If your dreams don't scare you, they're not big enough!"
- *Ellen Johnson Sirleaf*

"True Thanksgiving is Thanks Living."
- *Unknown*

Chapter 7

Ten Top Time Savers

For fun I asked my friends & family what their top time savers were! Here are the responses! I hope they help you save time!!!

1. Store some extra garbage bags in your garbage can under the current bag.
2. When loading your dishwasher separate the cutlery, when unloading you won't have to sort it.
3. Use a small tissue box to store small plastic reusable bags, very easy to retrieve.
4. Bedding - Place folded top and bottom sheet and one pillow case together, place in second pillow case, keeps everything together nicely.
5. Store several rolls of toilet paper on the top of your toilet tank in a gift bag suiting your bathroom décor.
6. Before baking or preparing a dish, read the recipe completely and bring out all the ingredients needed for that particular recipe.
7. Same as # 6, (but utensils).
8. Run a large safety pin through little socks before laundering to prevent loss (works on big ones too).
9. Before doing a major grocery shop, take some time to plan your meals for the week. That way you will only pick up the ingredients you don't have and you will save money on your grocery bill.
10. **ALWAYS PRAY TO START YOUR DAY.**

"God never wastes ANYTHING!... Those who see God's Hand in Everything, can best leave Everything in God's hands."
- *Unknown*

Chapter 8

Easy Peasy Recipes

Friendship grows in fellowship over a good food!
Here are some fun and easy recipes for
you and your friends to try!

I found these infusion recipes in various magazines.

<u>Infused waters and it's benefits</u>

4 cups green tea
2-3 mint leaves
2 slices of lime
Benefits: *fat burning, digestion, may relieve headaches,*
helps with congestion and acts as a breath freshener.

4 cups water
6 strawberries halved
1 sliced kiwi
Benefits: *cardiovascular health, immune system protection,*
blood sugar regulator and helps with digestion.

6 cups of water
1 cucumber (sliced)
1 lime (sliced)
1 lemon (sliced)
Benefits: *water weight management,*
bloating, appetite control,
Hydration and digestion.

4 cups of water
1 lemon (sliced)
1 lime (sliced)
1 orange (sliced)
Benefits: *Vitamin C source, immune defence,*
heart burn and aids digestion.

An apple a day keeps the doctor away!

SPUD PUFF

3 cups mashed potatoes
2 eggs (whisked with 1/3 cup sour cream)
1 heaping cup grated cheddar cheese
2 Tbsp parmesan cheese
2 Tbsp chopped chives
Salt and pepper to taste

Method:
- Preheat oven to 400° C
- Lightly grease muffin tin
- Add cheeses and chopped chives to the egg and sour cream mixture
- Add mashed spuds and mix well
- Spoon into muffin tin (slightly below top)
- Bake 25-35 minutes (until slightly brown)
- Remove from oven, cool about 5 minutes
- Serve with more sour cream

Enjoy!

"UN BORING ZUCCHINI"

2 large coarsely chopped onions,
2 large cans of whole tomatoes,
1 large bag of shrimp (de tailed)
1 medium zucchini (peeled and cubed)

Method:

- In a large pot begin to cook chopped onions
- Add tomatoes
- Add shrimp (remember, no tails)
- Add cubes of zucchini
- Cook until it comes to a full boil
- Serve with or over hot rice
- Servings 6-8

EASY 10 STEP SPAZONIA

1 small box uncooked spaghetti
1 large can (or jar) spaghetti sauce
1 can tomato soup
1 cup water
1 ½ cup shredded mozzarella cheese

10 simple step method:
- Grease 8x10 pan
- Mix sauce, soup, and water
- Spread ¼ of the mixed sauces into prepared pan
- Lay out ¼ of the dry spaghetti on top of sauce
- Sprinkle ½ cup grated cheese
- Repeat #3 and 4
- Sprinkle ½ cup shredded cheese
- Repeat #3 and 4
- Cover with last of grated cheese
- Bake at 375 °C for about 40 minutes (Or until spaghetti is cooked)

By Cindi

NUTRITIOUS "FLIP JACKS"

In a blender blend until smooth
1 cup raw or frozen spinach
½ cup orange juice
½ banana
1 cup any other fruit (fresh or frozen)
½ cup Vector cereal
1 Tbsp olive oil
1 egg

Method:

- Pour enough pancake mix into blended mixture (should be fairly thick but pourable)
- Heat frying pan or electric grill to moderate heat
- Cook jacks on one side until bubbles appear
- Flip jacks over (only once)
- Cook until golden brown on bottom
- Serve warm with your choice of topping
- Suggestions: Lemon juice and sugar, or fruit jam, or butter and syrup

By Robin L. McDonald

PISTACHIO SALAD DESSERT

1 package pistachio pudding
1 can crushed pineapple (drained)
1 cup mini marshmallows
1 large tub of cool whip

Method:

- Mix all together, chill about 2 hours.
- Simple and delicious.

By Janet H.

ANY FLAVOUR POUND CAKE

1 package (any flavour) cake mix
1 package instant pudding (a flavour
to compliment the cake)
4 eggs
½ cup cooking oil
1 cup water

Method:
- Beat above ingredients all together until well blended
- Pour into greased and floured loaf pan
- Bake at 350 °C on middle rack for about 45 minutes.
- Check for doneness with toothpick.

By Janet H

ORANGE MARSHMALLOW DESSERT

½ bag white marshmallows
1 cup orange juice
1 cup whipped cream

Method:
- Melt marshmallows in orange juice (on stove or in microwave)
- Cool until it resembles jelly
- Stir in whipped cream
- Chill at least 2 hours
- 6 Servings

LEMON LOVERS DELIGHT
(Only two ingredients!!)

1 box angel food cake
1 can (or jar) of lemon pie filling

Method:

- Preheat oven to 350 °C
- Line 8x12 pan with parchment (very important, it's super sticky!)
- Mix contents of two ingredients, whisk well (a little bit of foam should form)
- Pour into prepared pan
- Bake for 35-40 minutes

By Jo from Jo Cooks

ANY SEASON LITE DESSERT

1x1 litre tub of whipped topping
1 l large tin drained pineapple chunks
One package (any flavour) Jelly powder
Mix well and refrigerate overnight

Christmas- Red and or Green Jelly powder
Valentine's Day - Strawberry or Raspberry.
St. Patrick's Day - Lime Jelly powder.
Thanksgiving Day – Orange or Lemon Jelly powder.
Easter – Lemon or Grape Jelly powder.
Fun and Yummy!

BLUE HAVEN DESSERT

1x19 oz. can crushed pineapple
1 can of blueberry pie filling
1 yellow cake mix
1 Tbsp sugar
½ tsp cinnamon
1 cup butter
¾ cup chopped walnuts

Method:
- Grease a 9x13 cake pan
- Spread crushed pineapple (with juice) into pan
- Spread blueberry pie filling on to pineapple
- Sprinkle cake mix over mixture
- Combine sugar and cinnamon and sprinkle over cake mix
- Place thin slices of butter over all
- Sprinkle chopped walnuts over that.
- Bake at 350 °C for 35-40 minutes (until done)

By Janet H

CRAZY DAZY CAKE

½ cup milk
3 Tbsp butter
1 Cup brown sugar
1 Cup flour
1 Tsp baking powder
¼ Tsp salt
1 Tsp vanilla

Method (Part 1):
- Boil ½ cup milk with 3 Tbsp butter in a pot and set aside
- In a separate bowl, beat 2 eggs, add dry ingredients and vanilla

Method:
- Preheat oven to 350°
- Add these two mixtures together.
- Pour into greased pan (9x13)
- Bake for 25 minutes

Topping

8 Tbsp brown sugar
3 Tbsp butter
4 Tbsp milk
1 Cup shredded Coconut (optional)

Method:
- Boil together sugar, eggs and milk
- Add shredded Coconut (if desired)
- Pour mixture over cake and put back in oven until lightly browned

By Claudette W

IMPOSSIBLE COCONUT PIE

4 eggs
6 Tbsp butter
½ Cup flour
2 Cups milk
¾ Cup sugar
1 Tsp vanilla

Method:
- Blend all above ingredients for about 30 seconds
- Add 1 Cup of coconut
- Blend for another 30 seconds
- Pour mixture into 2 greased 8" pans or 1 x 10" pan
- Bake at 350° C for 45 minutes
- Servings 6-8

MOCK APPLE PIE

1 unbaked pie shell
30 Ritz crackers
2 Cups water
1 Cup sugar
½ Tsp cinnamon

Method:

- Combine water, sugar, and cream of tartar (Bring to a Boil)
- Drop in Ritz crackers and keep boiling for 5-6 minutes
- Pour mixture into pie shell
- Sprinkle with cinnamon and lemon juice
- Bake at 425°C for 15 minutes
- Add Crumb Topping (Ingredients to follow)
- Reduce heat to 375°C and bake for another 15-20 minutes

Crumb Topping

1 Cup fine crumbs from 25 Ritz crackers
½ Cup lightly packed brown sugar
1 Tbsp cinnamon
1/3 Cup melted butter
Combine all above.

Serve warm with cream or ice cream.
ENJOY

RHUBARB CRUMBLE

6 Cups Rhubarb
3 Tbsp flour
2/3 Cups sugar
½ Tsp cinnamon

Method:
- Preheat oven to 375°C
- Wash and prepare 6 cups of rhubarb (cut into ½ inch pieces)
- Combine 3 Tbsp flour, 2/3 Cup sugar, ½ Tsp cinnamon in a plastic bag.
- Throw rhubarb into bag and shake until fruit is all coated.
- Place in a 2-quart baking dish.

Topping

¾ Cup rolled oats
¾ Cup brown sugar
6 Tbsp flour
½ Tsp cinnamon

Method:
- Mix all together and sprinkle over fruit.
- Bake for 35 minutes or until rhubarb is tender and topping is golden.
- Cool 5-10 minutes before serving.
- Top with ice cream or cream.

(Can use gluten free flour for gluten free dessert as oatmeal has minimal gluten)

By Holly

DOG ICECREAM TREAT

3 ripe bananas
1 litre plain yogurt
1 Cup peanut butter
Blend all together thoroughly and pour
into ice cube trays and freeze!

(Cool treat on a hot day, kids like them too)

<u>WEED BE GONE</u>

1 Gallon water
2 Cups Epson salts
¼ Cup Dawn dish soap (blue original)
Just mix and spray after all dew has evaporated.

BAKED STONE

(Non-Toxic for kids)
Mix ½ Cup flour
¼ Cup salt
¼ Cup water (coloured if desired)
Knead dough
Roll out ½ - ¾ inches thick
Cut off edges by using a pot lid
Make desired print in center of circle
Bake at 200° C for about 3 hours.

Ideas For Prints

Childs's hand or foot, leaves or flowers,
or anything your heart desires.
Great kids craft.
HAVE FUN!

Trivia Tidbits!
How WD40 got its name - water displacement 40th attempt.

A jiffy is an actual unit of time - 1/100th of a second!

Chapter 9

<u>Recommended Reads</u>
(In My Opinion)

The Bible......Many authors, inspired by God

Debt Proof Your Marriage....Mary Hunt

The Purpose Driven Life....What on Earth am I here for? Rick Warren

Playground Prayers and Monkey Bar Meditations.... Dr. Rob Low
(Pics of my grandchildren in this book)

Forever 39 Mom....Lindsie Barrie
(Thank you for inspiring me Lindsie)

Praying the prayers of the bible.... James Banks

The Harbinger....Jonathon Cahn

A GOOD ESCAPE FROM REALITY IS
TO GET INTO A GOOD BOOK

Man is what he reads.
- *Joseph Brodsky*

"Just the knowledge that a good book is awaiting one at the end of a long day makes that day happier."
- *Kathleen Norris*

Chapter 10

Stay at Home Mom

I dedicate this to all the stay at home moms around the world. You have the most important job there is! And you're highly underpaid!

What do you mean you don't work outside the home?
Are you not a chauffeur? Are you not
a playground supervisor?
How about a sports team side line encourager?
A PTA representative?
A Sunday school teacher?
A volunteer?
Are you any of these?
All of these jobs are outside the home.
Never be afraid or ashamed to say you don't
have a regular job, you have many
many jobs, and are flexible to do them
while raising your children.
It is much more important to society and
community than any other job.
God bless you "stay at home mom"
For the wise choice you made in the job department.

Acronym for Mother
Mindful
Optimal
Tender
Helpful
Essential
Remarkable

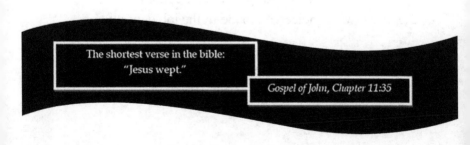

The shortest verse in the bible:
"Jesus wept."

Gospel of John, Chapter 11:35

Chapter 11

Alternate Acronyms

Some of these are my own creation! I hope you enjoy them!

BIBLE....Basic Instructions Before Leaving Earth.
BLAME....B....lame
BUSY....Being Under Satan's Yoke
COPD....Christ's Overall Protection Daily
COVID....Christ Offers Victory In Diseases
EGO.....Enormous Gloating Ongoing
FEAR.....False Evidence Appearing Real
FOMO....Fear Of Missing Out
GRACE.... Gifts Received At Christ's Expense
JOY.... Jesus, Others, Yourself
NO....Next Opportunity
SHAPE....Spirit, Heart, Abilities, Personality, Experience
THINK....is it **T**rue?
                 Helpful?
                 Inspiring?
                 Necessary?
                 Kind?

- Created By Berni

Instead of giving us what we can't handle, God helps us to handle what we are given.
-Unknown

Joy does not come from possessing everything, but from giving thanks for everything we possess.
- Unknown

Chapter 12

Puzzling Puzzles & Just Joking

For those days when you just need the lighter side of things!
(***All answers and explanations at the end of this chapter***)

Barefoot Boy *A Riddle*

A summer day in winter
The snow was raining fast
A Barefoot boy with shoes on
Sat standing in the grass.

What Do You Think?

1. How can you use these three different to's
(to, too, two) in one 7-word sentence?

2. What can go up a chimney down but
cannot go down a chimney up?

3. What goes "tic tic woof woof?"

Fishing Trip
(For the math lover)

Jimmy and Johnny went fishing and both caught fish.
As they were walking home Johnny said to
Jimmy, "If you give me one of your fish
I will have just as many as you." Jimmy
thought for a minute and then replied to
Johnny, "If you give me one of your fish,
I will have twice as many as you!"
How many fish did each of them catch?

Hardware Shopping

I went into the hardware store to buy a particular product. I found out that one would cost me $3. Then I found out that 20 would only cost me $6. Then lo and behold, I found out that 200 would only cost me $9. What was I buying?

Time

What occurs once in a minute, twice in a moment, and not once in 1000 years.

Bus Driver
(Math again, maybe)

You are driving a bus from city A to city B. You have 34 passengers in total. The passengers are all of ethnic groups aging from 18 to 65 years, the majority being between 30 and 40. There is only one scheduled stop between city A and city B where five passengers get off and seven new passengers get on. What is the age of the bus driver?

Ducks In A Row

If there is a duck in front of two ducks
and two ducks beside a duck,
How many ducks are there?

Jim versus John

Instead of John, I would like to call my
bathroom Jim; it sounds much better
when I say I went to the Jim (gym) this morning!!

Bra Sizes

Have you ever wondered what the A, B, C,
D, E, and F stand for in bra sizes?
A is for Absent
B is for blossoming
C is for coming along
D is for developed
DD is for delightfully developed
E is for exceptional
F is for fully developed
I'm sure that this is not true, but so good for a giggle!
(Friends and I came up with this one day)

<u>Auctioneers Tongue Twister</u>

Betty Botter bought some butter,
But she said the butter's bitter,
If I put it in my batter,
It will make my batter bitter,
So, she bought a bit of better butter,
Put it in her bitter batter,
Made her bitter batter better,
So, it's better Betty Botter bought a bit of better butter.
By Carolyn Wells
Taken from "The Jingle Book" in 1899

ANSWERS TO PUZZLES

Barefoot Boy...a warm day, sleet, boys name is Johnny Barefoot, crouching.

What Do You Think?.....I have two minutes to two too.

Up chimney/down chimney.... umbrella

Tic/woof.... watch dog

Fishing trip...Johnny caught 5, fish, Jimmy caught 7

Hardware Store... buying house numbers

Time....letter M

Bus Driver's age.... How old are you? You are the bus driver.

Ducks in a row....3 ducks   o
                        o o

More Trivia Tidbits

Butterflies taste with their feet.

An ostrich's eye is bigger than his brain.

Chapter 13

<u>What are the Odds</u>

(These stories are all non-fiction)

<u>Saved by A Tattoo!</u>

My husband decided he would like to get a new tattoo for his birthday. He designed a beautiful Maple Leaf / Thistle to represent his birthplace, Canada, and the country of his childhood, Scotland. The tattoo is beautiful; however, he did get a serious infection. So much so that he was hospitalized for intravenous over the next seven days. Well, obviously he wasn't able to work, so his whole work schedule was exact opposite of what it was originally.

Now if that hadn't occurred I would not be here today to write this story. As my husband's job took him away from home 10 days at a time, and because it was changed, he was home when I had my heart attack.

What are the odds?

God is so good!

By Berni Sharkey

<u>BBQ Bash</u>

I love to BBQ and my family loves it when I do. Now you can't have a good barbecue without a good sauce. As I was unscrewing the bottle top it slipped and fell and smashed all over the deck. A mess, yes! It also managed to hit my toe, so I felt some pain.

After getting it all cleaned up, I noticed it was gushing out of my sandal. It was then that I realized that it wasn't sauce, it was my blood. A piece of glass somehow got inside my sandal and cut my big toe severely. Needless to say, my husband took over the BBQing that day.

What are the odds?

Submitted by Lynda J.*(One of my longest friends)*

<u>Fourth Grade Dilemma</u>

My grandson, now 16, recollected an incident from 4th grade. He and some of his friends were in the hallway waiting for the teacher to come and unlock the classroom door. One of his buddies told a really funny joke and my grandson remembers laughing so hard that his head jolted backwards and ended up hitting the fire alarm. The bells were ringing and the Fire Department made it to the school in record time.

In the end all was well. Because of my grandson's usual good behaviour, the teacher believed it was truly an accident. All over a very funny joke.

What are the odds?

Submitted by Mike Sharkey (grandfather)

A Melting Moment For Mom

My youngest daughter was failing seventh grade so I decided I would keep her back the following year. As she was younger than her peers, and as her mom, I thought it would be in her best interest. I told her my plan, she was not too thrilled to say the least.

When year-end rolled around, the school held its awards evening. I went with my three children, as I thought my older two might be in the running. As they went from youngest to oldest, my younger daughters' class came before the other two.

Well, you can imagine my surprise when they called out my daughter's name. She received an award for "most improved student of the year. I was in awe, and so proud. She pulled her marks up from failing to a 60% average in the last quarter of the year. Needless to say, I did not hold her back and she went on to be an above average student.

My other two children did not receive any awards that year!

What are the odds?

By Berni Sharkey

The Events of Two Seniors

I was crossing a crosswalk one morning around 11:00 AM when all of a sudden, I felt something like metal hit me on my side. I found myself sitting in the middle of the road. My glasses fell off and my partial fell out of my mouth, miraculously, neither one was damaged. Two ladies came to my aid afraid that I might have gone into shock. Apparently, I was hit by a car driven by an 81-year-old lady who wasn't paying attention to the crosswalk. All kinds of help came. EMS took my vitals and asked questions regarding my pain. I was only a little sore on my side and my one knee.

Basically, when I was struck, I went flying over the vehicle to the other side. I was taken to emergency, had tests and x-rays, was given pain killers and then sent home.

After two years of treatment, mostly physio, and an injection at the tail bone site, things have settled down. Considering I weigh about 90 lbs. soaking wet, I believe I am very blessed to be alive. My guardian angel surely was with me.

What are the odds?

Submitted by Dorothy B. (Dear Friend)

P.S. The 81-year-old lady was fined and given 5 demerits!

The Love Story of Jimmy & Bonnie

Jimmy's first love was his first wife Marta. They were married for close to 30 years and had five children. Marta became ill and Jimmy became her caregiver.

The day came when Marta passed away and Jimmy was on his own. All his children were gone by this time, married with their own families. After several months the children saw how lonely their father was. They suggested he put himself out there for another wife. Daughter #3 made some suggestions: "go to the swimming pool, that way you will see what you're getting."

Another suggestion was to go to an evangelical church where they raise their hands, you'll see who's available. It was all in good humour, and he just stayed at home and waited.
One day he shared with daughter #4, that he would know the woman that was meant for him. She would be holding a single rose.

A few weeks passed and daughter #2 was at work at her assembly line job. Her boss called her into the office and asked if she would be interested in filling in for a woman that needed two weeks leave of absence. Daughter #2 was ecstatic, as it was like a promotion! The next day she was in with several senior ladies doing a different kind of job that she was not used to. A lovely lady named Bonnie was to be her trainer.

Within a couple of days Bonnie and daughter #2 got chatting. Bonnie shared that she had been widowed several years earlier, her paraplegic husband having passed. Daughter #2 gave her condolences, then proceeded to tell Bonnie about her widowed father, suggesting they meet.

Bonnie asked all sorts of questions. Does he drink? Does he smoke? After several more questions, she agreed to meet with Jimmy.

Daughter #2 called her father and they set a date. It would be for dinner at Jimmy's house (as he was an excellent cook). The big day came and daughter #2 picked Bonnie up. On the way Bonnie insisted on stopping at a florist. She came out with her purchase wrapped in a brown floral paper and they proceeded to Jimmy's house.

When Jimmy answered the door, daughter #2 introduced her dad to his blind date and then left. Awkward!

Bonnie handed Jimmy the floral package which he opened to find a single rose. The romance had begun, even though they didn't have a great deal in common. He loved playing cards, she loved bird watching. Over time Bonnie did learn to play cards, but Jimmy never did get into the bird watching.

They planned for a June wedding. In March of that same year daughter #2 had surgery, all seemed to go well, however two days later she passed away from an undetected blood clot. What sadness in the family as she left a husband and two children behind.

Jimmy and Bonnie came to the conclusion; daughter #2 was promoted for those two weeks at her job for the sole purpose of getting them together, so with sadness in their hearts they proceeded with their wedding plans.

It was a rough road for the first year or so as they really had to get used to each other. They had both been care givers in their previous marriages, so they both tended to be a bit bossy. Daughter #1 (who lived not too far away) was a little concerned for a time. A year went by and then another, things seemed to settle quite nicely and Bonnie came to be loved by her in-laws over time.

They celebrated their 25th wedding anniversary in June of 2019 and Jimmy celebrated his 97th birthday in September. On Valentine's Day the following year, Jimmy went home to Heaven to be with his first love.

He is greatly missed.

(This is a true story, only the names have been changed)

The promotion...
The introduction...
The rose...
What are the odds?...

Submitted by daughter #3

THE BLUE ROSES

It all actually began in the swimming pool. The water was cool and refreshing, the sun was shining gloriously, what a wonderful time we were having. My husband Mike and I decided to visit my one and only brother Brian, in Jomtien, Thailand. We stayed in one of his condos which was only about two hundred meters off one of the most beautiful beaches around. As much as I enjoyed our times at the beach, I preferred swimming in the pool at his condo. So sad, only four more days before we would have to board that plane and head back home to Canada.

When I first started swimming in the pool, I decided to do laps, something you really can't do in the ocean. I started at twenty laps and worked my way up to fifty. It was all good, expending all that energy I was able to indulge in all that amazing Thai cuisine and not feel guilty. Thirty-nine laps......What's this? I felt a small ripple across my chest, better cool it, too much exertion. It only lasted a few seconds so I wasn't overly concerned.

The following day Mike and I had decided to walk to the museum which was only about twelve blocks from the condo. Another ripple. I didn't tell Mike as I knew he would be all panicky, so I just asked if we could slow our pace a little and enjoy the stroll, we weren't in any hurry. The aquarium was amazing, so worth (what seemed to me) a long tedious walk.

We grabbed a 'bot' bus back to the condo, I quickly changed into my bathing suit and hit the cool pool. So refreshing after a hot excursion. Laps again. I didn't even make twenty when I felt the ripple again. What was going on? Once again, I didn't mention it to anyone, as we only had a couple of days left of holidays. I would go check it out once I got home.

The next afternoon we went to Nung Noot Gardens. Oh my, how magical! I was glad we decided to leave this particular outing for last, as it was the very best of all. If you are ever to go to Thailand and have a love for elephants this is a "Must see". The gardens themselves were so rich and bursting with color, the elephants were magnificent, so majestic! Mike was in awe, as that is his very favourite animal of all. What a wonderful way to end a fabulous holiday. Only a couple of small ripples today, I'm sure I'll be fine.

After dinner that evening, we said goodnight to my brother and went to our condo and decided to have some lovely time of intimacy. Shortly afterward the ripples started again, only they were much stronger and longer, and when the pain shot down my right arm, I had no choice but to tell Mike. We called Brian and he drove us to the hospital in Pattaya, which was only about fifteen minutes away. It was a very quiet ride to say the least. Mike was so angry with me for not telling him about these little episodes sooner, but too worried to give me grievance. Brian was very quiet also, and me, just silently praying the scripture "By his stripes I am healed and made whole" please Lord, don't let it be my heart.

The hospital in Pattaya was amazing! It was like entering a five-star hotel. Chandeliers, escalators, floral arrangements, crisp uniforms. Again, I say, amazing! As soon as we told them why we were there everything went into high speed. Seven hours later, plus three major types of heart testing, and nothing.

Of course, no ripples, no pains, during all this procedure. I almost felt like the doctor thought I was making it all up. The poor man didn't know what to tell me, other than to make sure to go and see my GP when I got back home.

Well, let me tell you, I was so relieved that it wasn't my heart. I was praying all the way to the hospital that it would not be my heart, and God heard those prayers.

The following day we were on the plane back to Canada. The flight was uneventful, other than it was long. Upon arriving home, I booked an appointment with my GP, only to be told it would be two weeks before I could get in to see him.

Once in, I was sent for all the tests again. Nothing showed up. My doctor concluded that it was likely chest muscle pain due to all the swimming I did on our holiday. Because the chest muscles were so worked, they were probably inflamed, so off to physio he sent me.

The funny thing was, the ripple sensations were very erratic. Some days there were none at all, other days I could have five or six, some mild, others not so mild. What was going on?

After several treatments of physio, and feeling no relief, I stopped going. Anytime I felt a ripple or any sensation in my chest I would stop whatever I was doing and just take a break. This went on for three months. I should have gone back to the doctor to ask him for further testing, as the ripples seemed to be getting stronger and more frequent.

A very dear friend of mine brought to my attention all the things I had on my plate at this particular time. I was organizing a charity auction, planning a 65th surprise birthday party for my husband, as well as being in the midst of the sale of our jewellery store. On top of all that, we had just recently sold our home and moved to a smaller house in a smaller community. Stress! Anxiety! Once all of these things were over, I'd be fine. One evening in mid-May, Mike and I were playing table tennis (which we played almost every night). Sometimes I could complete two or three games with no problem, however, this particular time a pain shot across my chest so bad that I had to lay down. It was the worst pain that I felt since all this started. Mike came into the bedroom to see how I was doing, I assured him I was alright, I just needed to rest for a while. All I remember was getting up to go to the bathroom. The next thing I see is my family standing around my bed. I was in the hospital; I had had a massive heart attack.

The following is not from my memory, but from what I was told:

Mike said he heard me grunt, then there was a thump. I had fallen off the toilet. He called 911 and they told him to get me on my back and straightened out as quickly as possible. By the time he had done that the paramedics were at the door. He said they were there in less than 10 minutes, but my heart had stopped, and they had to use the paddles two or three times. They kept the thumper on me all the way to the Mazenkowski Heart Institute at the University Hospital. I sure am grateful I was not awake for all of that.

I'm told I was kept completely sedated as they proceeded to put two stents in. I had two major blockages, one at eighty percent and one at ninety percent. I kept hearing my name being called, but as soon as they'd see me make any kind of move, they would sedate me again to make sure I remained perfectly still. Everything went well and I was moved from ICU into a ward with another woman. My first thought was" yellow walls" yuck! My least favourite color, but at least I knew the worst was over.

I can't remember if it was one or two nights later, but the pain in my ribs was excruciating and I couldn't fall asleep. I tossed and turned, but to no avail, sleep was not coming. A nurse came in doing her rounds, I waved to her and smiled, and commented that I couldn't sleep. She left, then came back about two minutes later with a pill. I don't know what kind of pill it was, but I fell into a sleep of the most vivid dreams. They were full of color and full of smells. I found myself in the midst of the most aromatic beautiful blue roses with white Baby's breath all around. It was exhilarating!

Then a thought came to me.

God, are you taking me home? It was so beautiful and so peaceful, and felt so perfect. Then I had another thought, Lord, I'm okay if you are taking me to be home with you, but you will really have to be with Mike. He will be so angry with You for a long time. Then I found myself sobbing and praying for my family.

The next thing I know, I wake up to beautiful sunny yellow walls. They didn't look as ugly as they had before, and I don't think I really hate yellow that much after all. I told everyone who came to visit me about my vivid dream, and how it seemed so real.

When I was finally discharged, my oldest daughter and my sister took me home. They insisted that I go right to bed, no ifs ands or buts. As I crawled under my covers, laying on my back, I could not believe my eyes. I called my sister and daughter and said, "look! Look at my room". My blue walls, my blue comforter, white stipple ceiling. I was surrounded by blue; my blue rose room, in my very own home. It was like God telling me, "Wake up and smell the roses!" Roses, by the way, are my husband's very favourite flower, maybe not blue, but roses never the less.

A very dear friend brought me a little folder filled with healing verses. As I read them for the first time, one jumped out at me, and it has become my personal favourite verse." I shall not die, but live, and declare the works of the Lord." Psalm 118:17

God has been so gracious, because if it hadn't been for an infection in my husband's leg from a recent tattoo, I would not have been here to tell my story.
What are the odds?

Love God, live life, and don't forget to smell the roses.

By Mike & Berni Sharkey

"A tree that looks at God all day and lifts her leafy arms to pray."
-By Joyce Kilman, from her poem "Trees."

We should always be thankful to our Angels!
-Berni S

Chapter 14

<u>Lovely Leftovers</u>

People say leftover stew is usually better than fresh, as it has time for those juices to truly soak in. My last chapter was supposed to be "What are the Odds", however, I found some bits and bobs afterward that I wanted to include, thus, "lovely leftovers." I hope you enjoy these at least as much as the first thirteen chapters.

Now for the leftovers...

"Enough is as good as a feast."
-Thomas Malory

"Be yourself, no one is more qualified."
- Fortune Cookie

"There is no hopeless situation, only people who have no hope."
- Clare Boothe Luce

"There are times when silence has the loudest voice."
- Leroy Brownlow (Today is Mine)

Quotes from "Older and Wiser"
Gretchen B. Dianda and Betty J. Hofmayer

"I will never be old. To me, old age is always 15 years older than I am."
- Bernard Baruch - age 85

"If you continue to work and to absorb the beauty in the world around you, you will find that age does not necessarily mean getting old."
- Pablo Casals - age 93

"We don't grow older; we grow riper."
- Pablo Picasso

"An archaeologist is the best husband any woman could have, the older she gets the more interested he is in her."
- Agatha Christie - age 64

"To be 70 years young is sometimes more cheerful than being 40 years old."
- Oliver Wendell Holmes Sr. Age - 80

Of course there are the average diseases we've all heard of....
but here are some..."not so" average diseases for a chuckle.....

Accelerator toe
Ashtray breath
Acidosis (sour stomach)
Bromodosis (sweaty foot odour)
Cosmetic skin
Dishpan hands
Enlarged pores
Homotosis (lack of attractive home furnishings)
Incomplete elimination
Middle age spread
Office hips
Pink tooth brush (bleeding gums)
Summer sluggishness
Tattle tale grey (dirt left on clothes
by mild laundry detergent)

These were found in Uncle John's Absolutely Absorbing
Bathroom Reader, by Uncle John

<u>Quotes from "Together with God"</u>
<u>"Psalms"</u>
<u>Excerpts from "Our Daily Bread"</u>

"Patience is a virtue that carries a lot of 'wait'."
"It's not how long you live that counts,
but how well you live."
"If we take care of our character, our
reputation will take care of itself."
"For every minute you are angry, you lose an
opportunity for 60 seconds of happiness."
"There is no legacy as rich as integrity."
"Time spent in prayer is always time well spent."
"Things looking down? Try looking up!"
"Don't just count your days; Make your days count."
"All creation is an outstretched finger
pointing towards God."
"If you know God's hand is in everything, you
can leave everything in God's hand."
"God takes heed of your every need."
"God's help is only a prayer away."

Please Remember These:
<u>Three Simple Words</u>
From A to Z

Always Be Prepared - Anything Is
Possible - Always Gives Thanks
Believe In miracles - Be A Blessing
Count Your Blessings
Do Your best - Dare To Dream
Expect The Unexpected - Enjoy Your Life
Forgive And Forget
Guard Your Reputation- God Is Faithful
Help The Needy
It Takes Teamwork
Just Be Yourself - Judge No One
Keep Yourself Humble - Keep It Simple
Lend A Hand - Love Conquers All
Maintain Self Control
Number Your Days
Owe No One
Put others first - Practice Makes Better
Quit Wasting Words
Rise And Shine- Read To Succeed
Set Your goals- Seize The day- Show Your faith
Train A child - Trust The Lord
Use Your talents-United We stand
Watch Your language - Words Can Hurt
You Can't Hide
ZZZ - Get enough Sleep

-Berni Sharkey

<u>Quotes from Mark Twain</u>

"Whenever you find you are on the side of
the majority, it is time to pause and
"REFLECT."
"It is easier to stay out then get out."
"There is no sadder sight than a young pessimist."
"Everything has a limit - iron ore
cannot be educated into gold."

"No one can make you feel inferior without
your consent."
- *Eleanor Roosevelt*

"See everything, overlook a great
deal and correct a little."
- *Pope John XX*

THE END

Acknowledgements:

My readers; thank you so much for purchasing this book. "Not Soup, but Great Mulligan Stew" is my first attempt at writing. It has been challenging at times, but very rewarding in so many ways. I hope you enjoy reading it as much as I enjoyed writing it.

I want to thank Rob Lowe and Lindsie Barrie, two friends who got themselves published. Unbeknownst to them, were my inspiration.

I want to thank my many contributors, without you there would be no book. Thank you so very much.

A huge hug and thanks to my daughter Robin, your patience, your love, and your computer skills. It has been such a learning curve for me and I could not have done it without you. May the Lord continue to bless you in all your endeavours.

I want to thank my family, especially my husband Mike, who stood by me, encouraged me, and loved me through this journey. So many times, I would tuck my notes deep into the file cabinet and he would ask "how's the book coming"? Thank you again my dear, wouldn't have done it without you.

Foremost, I want to praise and thank God, He was the ultimate One to carry me through to completion. To Him be the glory forever. Amen!

CPSIA information can be obtained
at www.ICGtesting.com
Printed in the USA
BVHW040026271121
622640BV00004B/44